Best Christmas Wishes

Joan & James Driver.

D0871394

PRINCETON IN SPRING

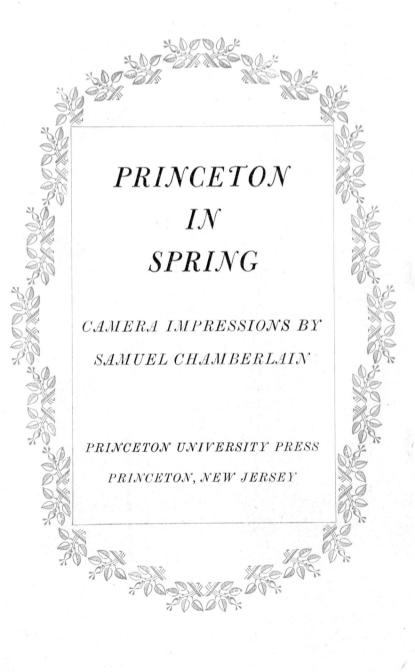

PRINCETON
IN
SPRING

CAMERA IMPRESSIONS BY
SAMUEL CHAMBERLAIN

PRINCETON UNIVERSITY PRESS

PRINCETON, NEW JERSEY

FOREWORD

THE freshness of Spring is heartening to any community, but this season is positively munificent to Princeton. Whether you spend a lifetime, four impressionable college years, or a mere weekend here, Princeton's radiance in Spring leaves an unforgettable impression. It is a moment for the sentimentalist, when the apprehension of June exams has not yet troubled the atmosphere. After the affront of a New Jersey winter, Nature suddenly becomes prodigal with gifts of sunshine and blossom. At this youthful season, somewhere between the first senior beer jacket and the last academic gown, the historic town is in its most beguiling mood. The moment is kind to the inquiring camera too, clothing the trees with a transparent screen of light foliage with none of the bareness of winter or the opacity of the summer leaf. Here is a propitious time for the presumptuous lensman to attempt to capture the haunting and affectionate image which is carried in later life by countless Princetonians.

Princeton is a community of varied accomplishments. An intellectual stronghold second to none in this country and the seat of one of our greatest universities, its name figured proudly during the Revolution. Its venerable relics and architectural treasures are many. It is pleasant to record that Princeton's historic and intellectual significance is today matched by its external beauty.

This volume has none of the aspirations of a guidebook or history. Princeton already has an exceedingly good guide, and its illustrious past was recently dramatized in a bicentennial pictorial history which remains a major achievement in its field. These accomplishments leave this book free for a more light-hearted pursuit—the search for an *impression* of Princeton's fresh indefinable charm in Spring. This may not be a very weighty assignment in view of the creative thought which churns behind these Gothic and Colonial façades, but the photographic image has its own contribution to make.

The camera's wanderings have a certain order and purpose. They begin with the earliest suspicion of foliage and end with a tumultuous burst of pink magnolia. They deal thoroughly with the University before shifting to Nassau Street and then to the outlying monuments of the historic town. No attempt has been made to include *all* of Princeton's noteworthy buildings, or to reinforce the pictures with lengthy explanatory captions. They must speak for themselves, with only the briefest legends to identify them. I hope that they speak with the warmth and eloquence which Princeton deserves.—SAMUEL CHAMBERLAIN

NASSAU HALL

THE
'79 TIGERS

UNIVERSITY CHAPEL

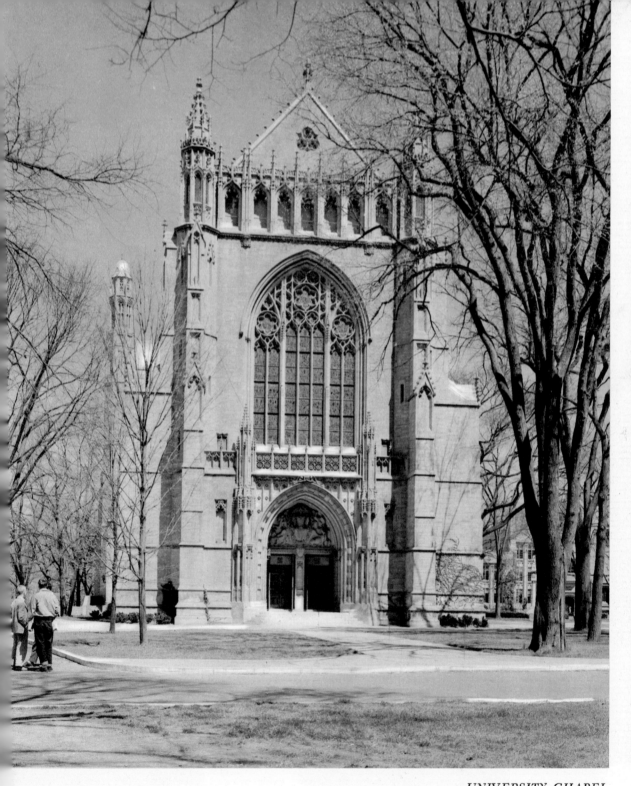

UNIVERSITY CHAPEL

SOUTH OF
THE CHAPEL

FIRESTONE
LIBRARY
AND CHAPEL

PYNE LIBRARY

STAFFORD LITTLE HALL

BLAIR
HALL

THROUGH

DODGE

GATEWAY

JOSEPH

HENRY

HOUSE

DINING HALLS AND HOLDER TOWER

HENRY HALL

FOULKE,

BLAIR,

LAUGHLIN

GRADUATE
COLLEGE

CLEVELAND TOWER

THOMSON COURT, GRADUATE COLLEGE

THE
CANNON
GREEN

NASSAU HALL

FITZRANDOLPH GATE

NASSAU HALL

STANHOPE HALL

FITZRANDOLPH GATE

REUNION HALL AND WEST COLLEGE

PYNE LIBRARY

LIBRARY AND CHAPEL

FIRESTONE LIBRARY

FIRESTONE LIBRARY

LIBRARY AND CHAPEL

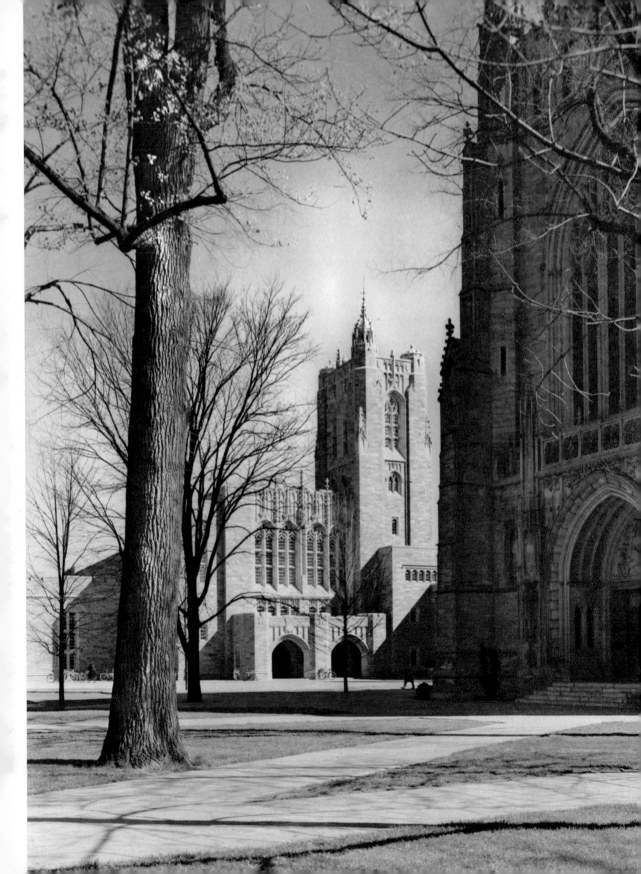

PYNE LIBRARY

MATHER SUNDIAL

WEST
COLLEGE

CLIO HALL

WHIG AND CLIO HALLS

DICKINSON AND MCCOSH HALLS

MCCOSH WALK

SOUTH OF CLIO HALL

ALEXANDER HALL

THE DEAN'S HOUSE

CAMPBELL HALL

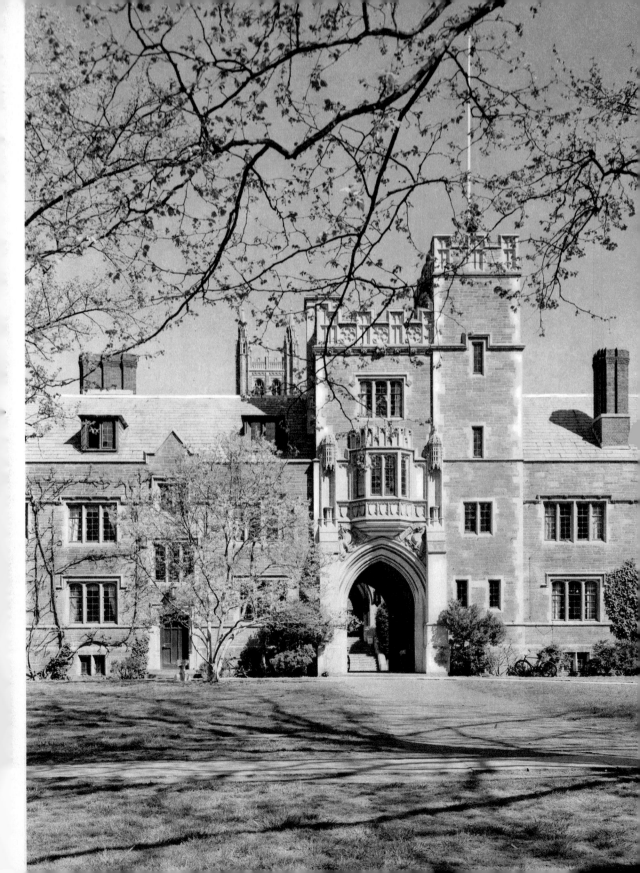

THE DEAN'S

HOUSE

HOLDER CLOISTER

LITTLE BLAIR ARCH

CAMPBELL

HALL

CUYLER
HALL

LOCKHART ARCH

BLAIR ARCH

DILLON GYMNASIUM

HOLDER TOWER FROM HAMILTON COURT

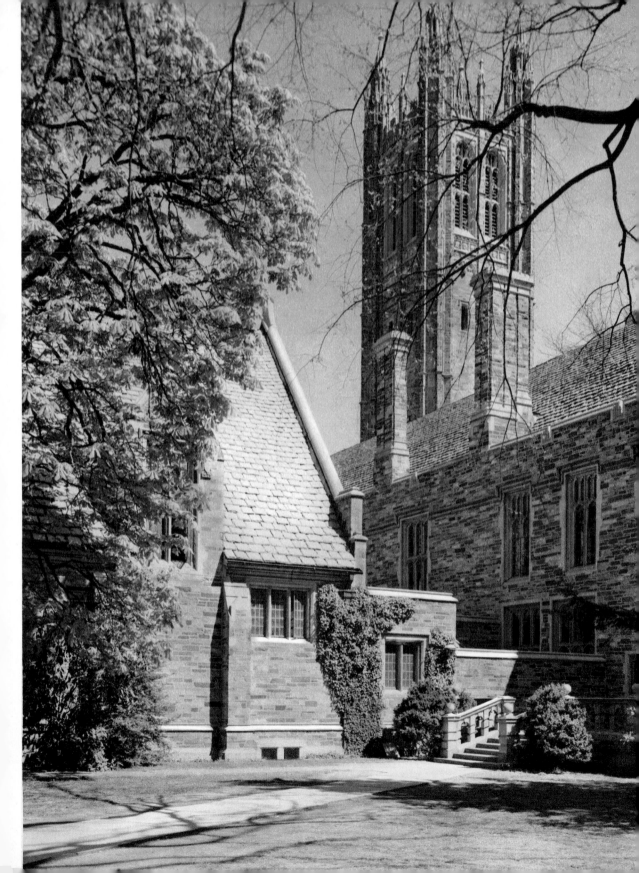

36

UNIVERSITY

PLACE

AND

LOCKHART

HALL

FOULKE-
HENRY
ARCHES

HAMILTON COURT

CAMPBELL HALL

PYNE
AND 1901
HALLS

DODGE GATEWAY AND HENRY TOWER

HOLDER TOWER

UNIVERSITY
DINING
HALLS

'79 HALL

DINING HALLS AND HOLDER TOWER

JOLINE HALL

ART
MUSEUM
AND
MC CORMICK
HALL

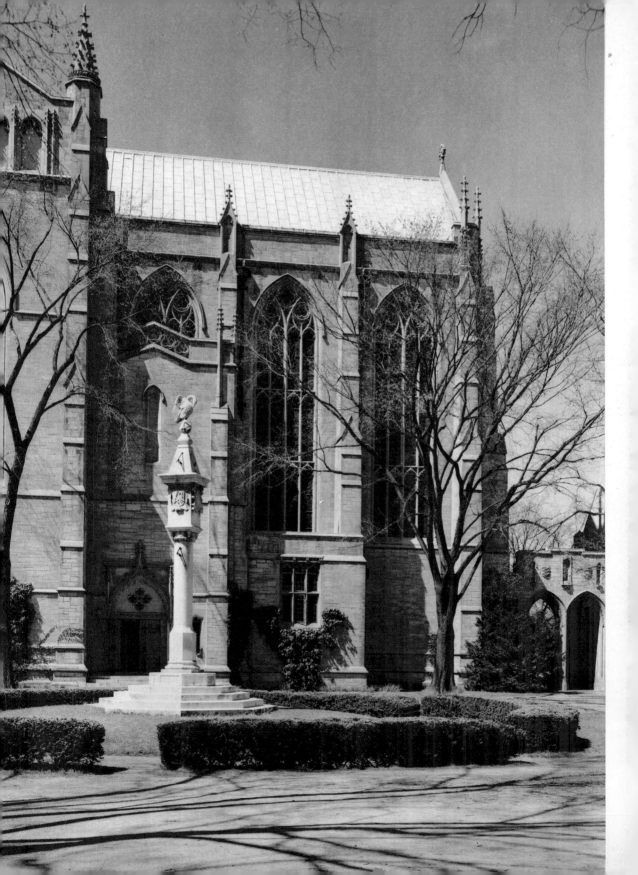

'79 ARCH

SUNDIAL, CHAPEL, ROTHSCHILD ARCH

UNIVERSITY

PRESS

COLLEGE ROAD FACULTY HOUSES

PRINCETON BATTLE MONUMENT

MORVEN

ALEXANDER
HALL
THEOLOGICAL
SEMINARY

72 LIBRARY PLACE

OLDEN COTTAGE

INSTITUTE FOR ADVANCED STUDY

OFF MERCER ROAD

THE
BARRACKS

WICKS HOUSE

LAWRENCEVILLE ROAD

TRINITY EPISCOPAL CHURCH

NASSAU STREET

PALMER SQUARE

BAINBRIDGE HOUSE (PUBLIC LIBRARY)

NASSAU
TAVERN

PROSPEC

MC CARTER
THEATER

OLDEN
MANOR

TUSCULUM

TUSCULUM

STONY
BROOK

HENRY
AND
1901
HALLS

BLAIR
HALL

BLAIR HALL

PALMER SQUARE

1887

BOATHOUSE

GRADUATE COLLEGE

GRADUATE COLLEGE

DEAN'S
GARDEN,
GRADUATE
COLLEGE

DEAN'S
GARDEN,
GRADUATE
COLLEGE

UNIVERSITY
CHAPEL AND
MURRAY-
DODGE

PRINCETON
INN

ACROSS

THE

FAIRWAYS